PARTY
in a
JAR

PARTY
in a
JAR

16 KID-FRIENDLY PROJECTS
for PARTIES, HOLIDAYS & SPECIAL OCCASIONS

VANESSA RODRIGUEZ COPPOLA

GIBBS SMITH
TO ENRICH AND INSPIRE HUMANKIND

Manufactured in Hong Kong in 2014 by Paramount

First Edition

18 17 16 15 14   5 4 3 2 1

Published by
Gibbs Smith
P.O. Box 667
Layton, Utah 84041

1.800.835.4993 orders
www.gibbs-smith.com

Designed by Michelle Thompson | Fold & Gather Design
Printed and bound in Hong Kong
Gibbs Smith books are printed on paper produced from sustainable PEFC-certified forest/controlled wood source. Learn more at www.pefc.org.

Library of Congress Cataloging-in-Publication Data

Coppola, Vanessa Rodriguez.
  Party in a jar : 16 kid-friendly projects for parties, holidays & special occasions / Vanessa Rodriguez Coppola. — First edition.
      pages cm
  ISBN 978-1-4236-3405-8
1. Handicraft for children. 2. Storage jars—Recycling.
3. Children's parties. I. Title.
  TT157.C64262014
  745.5083—dc23
                    2013027902

For Logan and Amelia, my greatest creations

CONTENTS

Encouraging creativity in your child is a wonderful way for them to explore the world in a new way. As someone who has a background in clinical social work, I've seen firsthand the positive impact crafting can have in the lives of children and even adults. It is therapeutic and will give your kids a positive lifelong outlet to turn to. Kids learn and communicate primarily through play. This book is a great tool to encourage that play and creativity. This is why I'm so passionate about it!

Allow children the space to make mistakes through their crafting. Their version of the project will be much more unique and special. It doesn't have to look perfect or even similar to the photos in the book. You may even be inspired to go back to your own childhood roots and craft alongside your child. Your kids will enjoy spending that quality time with you.

JARS

The great thing about all of the projects in this book is that they use something that most of us have plenty of in our home—JARS! Save your old peanut butter, pickle and other fun-shaped jars to use. If you are worried about breakage, you can stick with plastic jars for most of the projects. Mason jars can be easily found in most stores and are durable enough for the littlest of hands. I love the eco-friendliness of crafting with jars and it's the perfect opportunity to teach your kids about protecting the environment.

The easiest way to remove old labels off glass jars is to soak them in warm soapy water for 30–60 minutes. Most labels will easily come off at that point by scrubbing it with a sponge. If not, you can try placing a layer of peanut butter or Goo Gone adhesive removal over the sticky parts and letting it sit for 15–20 minutes before scrubbing in warm soapy water again.

DINO TERRARIUM JARS

—— Makes 10 decorated jars ——

Dinosaur fanatics will roar over these edible dino terrarium treats! They are just as fun to make as they are to eat. Your little paleontologists can help make these for a dinosaur-themed party or a special treat.

MATERIALS

10 (1-pint) Mason jars
1 (3.9-ounce) box chocolate pudding
1 (8-ounce) tub whipped topping
1 package chocolate-filled Oreo cookies
20 mint stems
1 cup Choco Rocks
10 miniature dinosaur toys

DIRECTIONS

1. Make pudding according to package directions. Mix in whipped topping. Chill in refrigerator for an hour.

2. Place 20 Oreo cookies in a large plastic bag and crush cookies.

3. Spoon ½ cup pudding mixture into Mason jars.

4. Stick 2 mint stems into the pudding in each jar.

5. Sprinkle crushed Oreo cookies on top of pudding.

6. Add in a few Choco Rocks and a miniature dinosaur toy to each jar.

Tip: Check out dinosaur books from the library and read them as the pudding mixture chills.

Note: Make sure kids separate the toy from the food before digging into their dino dessert.

MONSTER SLIME JARS

— Makes 6 decorated jars —

Kids will have a blast making homemade monster slime, stretchable green putty, and decorating a monster jar to hold the slime when not in use. You can have kids name their monsters and make up monster stories as they decorate their jars.

MATERIALS

6 baby food jars
pipe cleaners
scrapbook paper
2 (5-ounce) bottles clear school glue
googly eyes
craft glue
scissors or circle punches
acrylic paint
sponge brush
¼ cup water
green food coloring
1 teaspoon Borax
1 cup water

DIRECTIONS

1. Paint 6 baby food jar lids in your color of choice. Set aside to dry.

2. Shape pipe cleaner to look like monster arms and glue to the front of the jar.

3. Cut out 2 circles, 1 slightly larger than the other, from different-colored scrapbook paper. Glue circles to the jar, on top of the pipe cleaner, placing the larger circle behind the smaller circle.

4. Decorate jar using googly eyes, craft glue, scissors or circle punches, paint and sponge brush.

5. Pour 2 bottles of clear school glue into a large mixing bowl. Add ¼ cup water and 10 drops of green food coloring, mix well.

6. Dissolve 1 teaspoon of Borax in 1 cup of water and add to glue mixture. Use your hands to mix and knead until a solid glop is formed.

7. Store slime in monster jar when not in use.

Tip: Be creative and use different sizes of googly eyes and different paper and pipe cleaner colors. You can add some yarn hair, fangs or maybe even some antennaes.

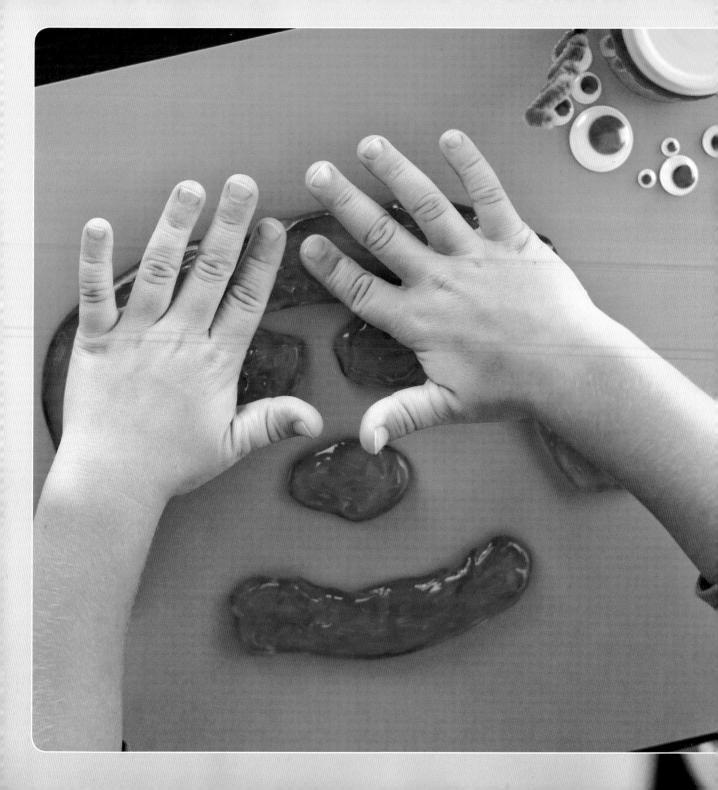

—— Makes 14 decorated jars ——

These cute little bumblebee treats are easy to make and are sure not to sting. Make a swarm of bees to share with friends. They'll be buzzing about this dessert all day!

MATERIALS

14 (½-pint) Mason jars
1 box chocolate cake mix
½ cup sour cream
1 (3.9-ounce) box chocolate pudding
non-stick cooking spray
sharp knife
5 (20-ounce) cans crushed pineapple
14 yellow cupcake liners
14 black pipe cleaners
craft glue
28 miniature yellow pom-poms
28 medium googly eyes

DIRECTIONS

1. Make chocolate cake batter according to box directions, substituting ½ cup of sour cream for ½ cup water.

2. Make chocolate pudding according to box directions. Mix with cake batter.

3. Spray Mason jars with non-stick cooking spray and fill jars half full with cake batter. Bake according to cake box directions or until cake is completely cooked through the center. Allow to cool.

4. Once cake is cooled, it should slide right out of the Mason jar. Slice cake in thirds, trimming and discarding the uneven top piece (adults only).

5. Place a layer of cake in the jar, layering ¼ cup of crushed pineapple on top and repeating until the jar is full.

6. Place lids on the jars and cupcake liners over the lids. Twist a pipe cleaner around the cupcake liner, with the ends of the pipe cleaners twisted up to look like antennaes. Glue 2 pom-poms to the ends.

7. Glue 2 googly eyes to the center of the pipe cleaner.

Tip: Wash your Mason jars after baking cake in them, before you create your bees, so you can better see the bubble bee layers.

PRINCESS SMOOTHIE JARS

—— Makes 5 decorated jars ——

This smoothie recipe is fit for a princess, and a handmade tutu jar is the perfect way to drink it. Kids can also craft a princess wand out of fruit and enjoy a healthy snack on the side.

MATERIALS

1 roll pink tulle
1 roll pink ribbon
5 (1-pint) Mason jars
2 cups frozen strawberries
1 banana
½ cup milk or ice
16 ounces strawberry sorbet
pineapple
star cookie cutter
skewers
grapes

DIRECTIONS

1. Cut tulle into 2 x 6-inch strips. You will need approximately 50 strips for each tutu.

2. Cut a piece of ribbon long enough to wrap around a Mason jar with enough slack to tie it around the jar.

3. Fold the tulle strips in half and double knot them around the ribbon, bunching the tulle together to form a tutu. Attach the tutu to the jar, using the excess ribbon. Repeat steps 1–3 for additional tutus.

4. Add frozen strawberries, banana, milk and strawberry sorbet to a blender and blend until creamy. Pour into tutu jars.

5. Shape pineapple slices into stars using a star cookie cutter. Add pineapple stars to the top of skewers with several grapes underneath to make princess wands.

Tip: The tutu, while easy to make, will take some time to complete. You may want to make the tutu well in advance before starting your smoothie.

Note: Make sure kids are careful with the sharp end of the skewer. You can use a straw instead of a skewer for added safety.

PATRIOTIC POPCORN JARS

—— Makes 10 decorated jars ——

Celebrate the Fourth of July with red-white-and-blue-colored popcorn in a jar. Kids will have fun coloring their popcorn before enjoying this festive snack under the fireworks.

MATERIALS

10 (1-pint) Mason jars
1 cup popcorn kernels
3 sealable plastic bags
½ teaspoon blue edible color dust
½ teaspoon red edible color dust
10 festive cupcake liners
jute or string

DIRECTIONS

1. Pop 1 cup of popcorn kernels according to package directions.

2. Divide popped popcorn into 3 large sealable plastic bags.

3. Add ½ teaspoon blue edible color dust in one bag, seal and shake until the popcorn is completely colored. Add ½ teaspoon red edible color dust in another bag, seal and shake until the popcorn is completely colored. Leave the last bag of popcorn uncolored.

4. Layer the popcorn in jars starting with the blue popcorn, adding the uncolored white popcorn and then the red.

5. Place lids on the jars and cover the lids with a festive cupcake liner, tying it in place with jute or string.

Tip: You can find edible color dust in the cake-decorating aisle of most craft supply stores.

PUMPKIN PLAY DOUGH JARS

—— Makes 9 decorated jars ——

Kids can make a batch of play dough and hand it out to trick-or-treaters instead of candy on Halloween. This pumpkin-scented play dough smells good enough to eat, but it's just for playing with.

MATERIALS

9 (6-ounce) baby food jars
green acrylic paint
sponge brush
3 cups flour
1½ cups salt
6 teaspoons cream of tartar
3 tablespoons vegetable oil
3 cups water
6 teaspoons pumpkin spice
2 teaspoons cinnamon
30 drops yellow food coloring
10 drops red food coloring
parchment paper
1 (8½ x 11-inch) black sticky felt sheet
scissors
9 green pipe cleaners
pencil

DIRECTIONS

1. Paint jar lids with 2–3 coats of green acrylic paint and set aside to dry.

2. Mix flour, salt, cream of tartar, oil, water, pumpkin spice, cinnamon and food coloring over medium heat on the stove in a large pot, constantly stirring for 5–10 minutes until the ingredients turn into a dough consistency (adults only).

3. Allow dough to cool on a piece of parchment paper. Once cool enough to touch, kids can knead the dough until no longer sticky.

4. Cut pumpkin faces out of black sticky felt and stick on jars.

5. Place approximately 2 cups of dough into each jar and place the painted lids on the jars.

6. Attach a green pipe cleaner around the jar lids and curl the ends around a pencil to look like vines.

7. Kids can use a rolling pin to flatten play dough, and cookie cutters to cut out festive shapes.

Tip: Store play dough in its jack-o'-lantern jar when it isn't being played with so it doesn't harden. Play dough should last for at least 6 months.

—— Makes 1 decorated honey bear jar ——

This is a great upcycled project, perfect for Father's Day! Kids can make pop a special gift by turning an old honey bear jar into his look-a-like, complete with a bowtie and mustache. Fill the jar with dad's favorite treats, and once the jar is empty, it can be used as a pencil holder.

MATERIALS

empty honey bear jar
craft glue
2 medium googly eyes
scissors
1 (8½ x 11-inch) colored sticky felt sheet
   (any color)
3 buttons
1 (8½ x 11-inch) black sticky felt sheet
dad's favorite snacks

DIRECTIONS

1. Wash and dry empty honey bear jar.

2. Glue googly eyes to the bear's head.

3. Cut a bowtie shape out of the colored sticky felt and stick it to the bear's neck.

4. Glue a button to the middle of the bowtie and 2 additional buttons under it.

5. Cut a mustache shape out of the black sticky felt and stick it under the bear's nose.

6. Fill the jar with dad's favorite snacks.

Tip: Fill the jar with nuts, seeds, raisins, pretzels or candy. Kids can also fill the jar with reasons why they love their dad.

—— *Makes 8–9 eggs for 2 jars (4 eggs per jar)* ——

Kids won't fight bath time with this homemade bath bomb recipe. The best part is that they are shaped like Easter eggs and kids can decorate an Easter bunny jar to store them in. Hop to it!

EGG BATH BOMB MATERIALS

1 cup baking soda
½ cup citric acid
½ cup cornstarch
¼ teaspoon borax (an emulsifier)
2½ tablespoons almond oil
¾ tablespoon water
½–1 teaspoon lavender essential oil
¼ teaspoon vitamin E oil
9 plastic Easter eggs
witch hazel
spray bottle
cupcake baking pan
fluffy towel

EASTER BUNNY JAR MATERIALS

Makes 1 decorated jar

1 (1-pint) Mason jar
pink acrylic paint
sponge brush
scissors
white cardstock
pink cardstock
craft glue
3 pink pipe cleaners
1 medium pink pom-pom
2 medium googly eyes
1 large white pom-pom

DIRECTIONS

1. Combine baking soda, citric acid and cornstarch together until smooth.

2. Mix in borax, almond oil, water, essential oil and vitamin E oil to the dry ingredients.

3. Separate the plastic Easter egg halves and pack each side with the mixed bath bomb ingredients.

4. If the ingredients aren't sticking together, place ¼ cup of witch hazel in a spray bottle and lightly mist the ingredients 1–2 times.

5. Allow the halves to harden for 10 minutes. Gently remove bath bombs out of their egg molds. Attach the halves together, lightly spritzing one side with witch hazel to act as "glue." Place bath bombs on top of a cupcake-baking pan, covered by a fluffy towel. Allow to harden completely overnight.

6. Paint the Mason jar lid with 2–3 coats of pink acrylic paint. Allow to dry.

7. Cut Easter bunny ear shapes with flaps at the bottom out of white cardstock, with pink cardstock for the inner ear. Glue the flaps to the top of the Mason jar lid.

8. Cut 3 pink pipe cleaners in half and glue to the middle of the jar, arranging them to look like whiskers. Glue a pink pom-pom in the center of the whiskers for the nose.

9. Glue 2 googly eyes above the pom-pom nose and a large white pom-pom to the back of the jar for the tail.

10. Place 4 bath bombs in the bunny jar.

Tip: If you are having a difficult time getting the bath bomb out of the mold, lightly squeeze the mold and it should pop out.

—— Makes 3 decorated jars ——

Calling all beach bums! Your kids can make their own miniature beach jars and enjoy them for a healthy snack too! This applesauce recipe contains no added sugar and kids will enjoy making it from scratch. These jars would be fun to make at a beach-themed birthday party.

MATERIALS

5 medium peeled and cored apples
1 teaspoon nutmeg
2 teaspoons cinnamon
¼ cup water
3 (4-ounce) jelly jars
brown sugar
3 Teddy Graham bear cookies
3 gummy Life Savers
3 miniature cocktail umbrellas
3 small gumballs

DIRECTIONS

1. Place apples, nutmeg, cinnamon and water in a pot. Cover and cook over medium heat for 20 minutes, stirring occasionally (adults only). Mash with a fork or adults can place apples in a food processor until smooth.

2. Spoon equal amounts of applesauce into jelly jars. Lightly sprinkle applesauce with brown sugar.

3. Place Teddy Graham bears inside of gummy Life Savers and place on top of applesauce.

4. Place miniature umbrellas and gumballs on top of the applesauce as well.

Tip: You'll have to stretch the gummy Life Saver a bit to get it over the Teddy Graham cookie.

GRASS HAIR FUNNY FACE JARS

— Makes 1 decorated jar —

These grass hair funny face jars are the perfect project for kids of all ages. Kids will enjoy tending to their grass each day and watching for growth. They can get creative with their funny faces and cut out fun accessories to decorate their jars.

MATERIALS

1 (½-pint) jar
potting soil
grass seed
adhesive googly eyes
kid-friendly scissors
adhesive felt
watering can

DIRECTIONS

1. Fill the jar an inch from the top with potting soil. Sprinkle a layer of grass seed on top of the soil and sprinkle with another layer of potting soil half an inch from the top of the jar.

2. Attach adhesive googly eyes to the jar.

3. Cut mustaches, bowties, lips and other funny facial features out of adhesive felt and attach to the jar.

4. Heavily water your seeds daily until they start sprouting, at which point you can switch to light watering every other day. You'll also want to keep your jar in a sunny location in your home.

5. Once the grass "hair" starts growing, you can give it a trim with scissors.

Tip: It will take 1–2 weeks before the grass starts looking like "hair." If you are planning on making these at a party, you may want to plant the grass ahead of time and allow the children to decorate the jars with funny faces.

—— Makes 4 decorated jars ——

This is the perfect hands-on activity for kids! They can help measure and pour ingredients before shaking them together to create colorful rice. You may want to do this activity outdoors as it can get messy and the alcohol used to dye the rice will smell.

MATERIALS

4 (25-ounce) jars
plastic freezer bags
12 cups white rice
2 tablespoons alcohol (per bag)
20 drops food coloring (per bag)
parchment paper
red acrylic paint
sponge brush
green cardstock
scissors
craft glue
canning funnel

DIRECTIONS

1. Fill 6 plastic freezer bags with 2 cups of white rice each.

2. Add 2 tablespoons of alcohol and 20 drops of red food coloring to the first bag. Seal the bag and shake until the rice is completely coated and colored. Spread out rice on parchment paper and allow to dry for 2–3 hours.

3. Repeat step 2 to make yellow-, orange-, green-, blue- and violet-colored rice. To make orange rice, use 10 drops of yellow and 10 drops of red food coloring. To make violet, use 10 drops of red and 10 drops of blue food coloring.

4. While the rice is drying, paint the jar lids with 2–3 coats of red acrylic paint using a sponge brush.

5. Cut 4 shamrocks out of green cardstock and attach them to the front of the jars using craft glue.

6. Once the rice is dry, place a canning funnel on top of the first jar and layer rice: ½ cup of violet rice, ½ cup blue rice, ½ cup of green rice, ½ cup of yellow rice, ½ cup of orange rice and ½ cup of red rice. Repeat for remaining jars.

Tip: Once kids are done with their St. Patrick's Day jars, empty the contents into a small bin for additional sensory fun. Add small scoops or containers to play with in the bin.

—— *Makes 1 decorated jar* ——

These space nightlights are out of this world! Little astronauts will enjoy decorating jars with tissue paper stars that illuminate in the dark. In addition to stars, your child can cut out planets or add constellations to his or her jar.

MATERIALS

tissue paper
scissors or star punch
1 (1-pint) Mason jar
sponge brush
Mod Podge
battery-operated LED tea light

DIRECTIONS

1. Cut tissue paper into star shapes or use a star punch. You'll need approximately 20 stars to cover the entire jar.

2. Use a sponge brush to lightly coat the jar with Mod Podge. Attach stars to the jar and add another light coat of Mod Podge on top of the stars. Allow the jar to dry.

3. Place an LED tea light candle inside of the jar to illuminate.

Tip: Try color-changing LED lights for a fun effect. You can find LED lights in bulk on eBay.

—— Makes 1 decorated jar ——

Save old peanut butter jars and upcycle them into piggy banks. Kids can learn about counting and saving money with this fun craft. This is a great project for adults and kids to work on together.

MATERIALS

pink acrylic paint
1 (18-ounce) peanut butter jar
tin foil or thick cardboard
4 medium corks
sponge brush
1 pink pipe cleaner
pencil
2 large googly eyes
hot glue gun
craft glue
scissors
1 sheet dark pink adhesive felt
2 medium black pom-poms
light pink cardstock

DIRECTIONS

1. Squirt ½ inch of pink acrylic paint into the bottom of a clean and empty peanut butter jar. Swirl the paint until it covers the entire inside of the jar. Place the jar upside down on tin foil. Move the jar around the tin foil or thick cardboard every 10–15 minutes for an hour or until all of the excess paint is gone. Allow to fully dry overnight.

2. Paint the peanut butter lid and corks with 2–3 coats of pink acrylic paint, using a sponge brush. Allow to dry.

3. Twirl a pink pipe cleaner around a pencil to look like a tail and attach it to the bottom of the jar using hot glue (adults only).

4. Hot glue the 4 corks to the side of the jar to look like feet (adults only).

5. Attach googly eyes to the lid using craft glue. Cut a 1-inch circle out of dark pink adhesive felt and attach it to the center of the lid. Use craft glue to attach 2 pom-poms to the center of the felt circle to look like a snout.

6. Cut ear shapes out of light pink cardstock, using dark pink adhesive felt for the inner ears. Create a small fold at the bottom of each ear to attach to the lid as shown in the photo.

Tip: Use a sponge brush to reach areas that haven't been fully coated with paint inside of the jar.

THANKFUL TURKEY CENTERPIECES

—— Makes 1 decorated jar ——

Kids can collect pinecones to make up a batch of homemade scented pinecones for their turkey centerpiece jars. These jars will look and smell great sitting in the middle of a Thanksgiving table, and it can be reused for years to come.

MATERIALS

pinecones
large freezer bag
spray bottle with water
cinnamon essential oil
1 extra-large pickle jar
scissors
brown, green, blue, yellow and red
   adhesive felt
small adhesive googly eyes

DIRECTIONS

1. Place pinecones in a large freezer bag. Add water to the spray bottle and mix in several drops of cinnamon essential oil. Generously spray the pinecones. Seal the freezer bag overnight. Allow the pinecones to dry and then place them inside of the pickle jar.

2. Trace your child's hand onto the green, blue, yellow and red adhesive felt. Cut out the handprints and attach to the jar as shown in the photo.

3. Cut a 1-inch and 3-inch circle out of brown adhesive felt and attach to the jar, as shown in the photo. Add a small yellow triangle to the smaller circle, as shown in the photo. Attach 2 small googly eyes above the triangle.

Tip: If you don't live in an area where pinecones can be readily found, most craft stores sell already scented pine cones around the holidays that you can use to fill your jar with.

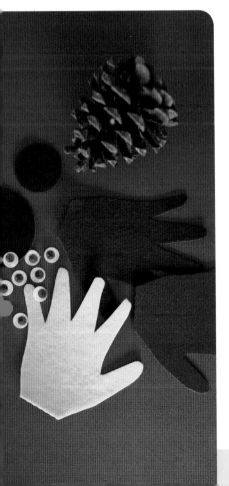

—— Makes 2 decorated jar candles ——

This is a fun holiday project for adults and kids to work on together. Kids can bring their snowman candles to life with some rickrack, sticky felt, pom-poms and googly eyes. Make up a batch of these jolly snowmen to use as gifts. Kids can skip the candle steps and use these snowmen jars as pencil holders.

MATERIALS

2 candlewicks
tacky glue
1 pound microwavable candle wax
microwave-safe bowl
candle fragrance (optional)
2 (½-pint) jars
sponge brush
scissors
small googly eyes
small black pom-poms
red rickrack
orange adhesive felt
black acrylic paint

DIRECTIONS

1. Attach the wicks to the bottom of the jars using tacky glue. Allow to dry.

2. Microwave wax in a microwave-safe bowl, according to the package directions. Add in desired candle fragrance before microwaving.

3. Pour the wax into the jars (adults only). You can place a sponge brush on top of the jar and drape the top of the wick over the handle to make sure the wick stands straight up.

4. Once the wax hardens, cut the wick down to ½ inch above the wax.

5. Attach googly eyes, pom-poms and rickrack to the jar, as shown in the photo.

6. Cut small triangular noses out of orange adhesive felt and attach to the jar, as shown in the photo.

7. Paint the lid with 2–4 coats of black acrylic paint and allow to dry.

Tip: Please make sure that a lit candle is out of reach of children and never left unattended.

PIZZA IN A JAR

—— Makes 9 decorated jars ——

Budding chefs will enjoy making their very own personal-sized pizza in a jar. Kids can get creative with the ingredients and add in veggies or other favorite pizza toppings before sticking it in the oven. You'll want to use wide-mouth jars for this project to make scooping out the ingredients easy for kids.

MATERIALS

9 (½-pint) wide-mouth jars
cooking spray
¼ cup pizza dough per jar
2 tablespoons pizza sauce per jar
mozzarella cheese
mini pepperonis
baking sheet

DIRECTIONS

1. Preheat oven to 400 degrees F.

2. Spray the jars with a light coat of cooking spray.

3. Place ¼ cup pizza dough at the bottom of each jar. Spoon 2 tablespoons of pizza sauce on top of each jar. Sprinkle cheese and mini pepperonis on the top.

4. Place jars on a baking sheet and bake for 400 degrees F for 15–20 minutes or until the pizza dough is fully cooked (adults only).

5. Allow the jars to completely cool before eating with a fork.

Tip: I recommend using the frozen pizza dough that can be found in a can in the frozen aisle of a grocery store.

ACKNOWLEDGMENTS

Thank you to my husband for believing in me and helping me chase my dreams. Thank you to Logan and Amelia for inspiring me and challenging me to be better at all that I do.

Thank you, Mom and Dad, for your unconditional love and support, whether it be a dance recital or a book. Thank you to my grandmother for introducing me to crafting at a young age and planting a creative seed inside of me. Thank you to Nicole for your friendship and keeping me sane during this process. Thank you to all of my family and friends for your encouragement; it means the world to me.

Many thanks to my editor, Hollie Keith, and the Gibbs Smith team for their guidance and faith. Thank you to Jen for your beautiful photography. A special thank-you to the readers of my blog, www.seevanessacraft.com. This book wouldn't exist without you.

Social worker turned stay-at-home mom and author **Vanessa Rodriguez Coppola** lives in Arizona with her husband, Rich, and two children.

Vanessa attended New Mexico State University where she earned a bachelor's degree in Social Work and Journalism Mass Communications. She also attended The University of Texas at Austin and earned a master's degree in Social Work.

She is passionate about inspiring creativity in others. When not busy with her kids, Vanessa can be found in her organized mess of a craft room and blogging about her love for glitter and hot glue at SeeVanessaCraft.com.